The Symbolism Of Astrology

Alan Leo

CHAPTER IV.

The Symbolism of Astrology.

The Planets. Circle ○, half-circle ☽, and cross +. These three symbols comprise the whole of the symbology connected with the planets, and according to their arrangement we know the name of each planet and understand its nature, for these three symbols represent Spirit, Soul and Body. Therefore, whenever we study the circle ○ we know that we are studying that which relates to Life and Spirit, the ☽ that which relates to Soul or Mind, and the + that which relates to the Body or Form. From time immemorial the symbols of the planets have been as follows :—

Symbol	Name
☉	Sun
☽	Moon
☿	Mercury
♀	Venus
♂	Mars
♃	Jupiter
♄	Saturn
♅	Uranus
♆	Neptune

Thus we have seven planets; with Sun, Moon, and Earth; these three being considered as planets for astrological purposes.

By becoming familiar with the symbols, we know at sight what they represent; and, in blending them one with another, we learn the nature of their influence upon human destiny.

The symbols of the planets form the Alphabet of Astrology, therefore it is necessary to learn each symbol so that it may be used instead of the name.

The Signs of the Zodiac. The symbology of the twelve

signs of the Zodiac is not quite so simple, and appears to have been more or less distorted since its original conception. It is probable that the various portions of the human body were originally portrayed in the twelve symbols of the zodiacal signs, and even now it requires very little stretch of the imagination to see the marking of the body in the twelve signs. The sign Aries (♈), representing the head and face, is a miniature diagram of the nose and eyebrows; Taurus (♉) represents the neck and throat; Gemini (♊) the lungs; Cancer (♋) the breasts; Leo (♌) the heart; Virgo (♍) the bowels; Libra (♎) the reins and kidneys; Scorpio (♏) the secret parts; Sagittarius (♐) the thighs; Capricorn (♑) the knees; Aquarius (♒) the ankles; Pisces (♓) the feet.

These twelve signs are divided into Northern and Southern signs as follows:—

NORTHERN OR ASCENDING SIGNS.			SOUTHERN OR DESCENDING SIGNS		
Symbol.	*Name.*		*Symbol.*	*Name.*	
1. ♈	Aries	Spring Signs	7. ♎	Libra	Autumn Signs
2. ♉	Taurus		8. ♏	Scorpio	
3. ♊	Gemini		9. ♐	Sagittarius	
4. ♋	Cancer	Summer Signs	10. ♑	Capricorn	Winter Signs
5. ♌	Leo		11. ♒	Aquarius	
6. ♍	Virgo		12. ♓	Pisces	

The signs always remain in the above order from ♈ to ♓. The symbols should invariably be written instead of the names.

The Signs of the Zodiac may in a sense be said to form the basis of the whole horoscope, and the more thoroughly they are mastered the easier will the reading of the horoscope become. The following table, reprinted from p. 8 of Manual I., will be found useful for reference.

THE SIGNS OF THE ZODIAC.

	NORTHERN		*opposite to*		SOUTHERN		
Spring	1. ♈ Aries	(+ *c.* F.)		(A. *c.* +)	Libra	♎ 7.	*Autumn*
	2. ♉ Taurus	(—*f.* E.)		(W. *f.* —)	Scorpio	♏ 8.	
	3. ♊ Gemini	(+ *m.* A.)		(F. *m.* +)	Sagittarius	♐ 9.	
Summer	4. ♋ Cancer	(— *c.* W.)		(E. *c.* —)	Capricorn	♑ 10.	*Winter*
	5. ♌ Leo	(+ *f.* F.)		(A. *f.* +)	Aquarius	♒ 11.	
	6. ♍ Virgo	(— *m.* E.)		(W. *m.* —)	Pisces	♓ 12.	

F., Fiery E., Earthy A., Airy W., Watery
c., cardinal *f.*, fixed *m.*, mutable
+ positive — negative

1, 2, 3 = *Intellectual Trinity* 7, 8, 9 = *Reproductive Trinity*
, 5, 6 = *Maternal Trinity* 10, 11, 12 = *Serving Trinity*

In the ensuing delineation the term "native" is employed, as in all astrological literature, to denote the individual whose temperament is under discussion. It has of course no relation to *nationality*, as is the case when used in its usual sense.

The separate influence of each sign may be briefly summarised as follows :—

The Nature of the Twelve Signs.

I. *Aries* (♈) is a fiery and cardinal sign, and like the first house governs the head. This sign governs the head and face in the physical body; the impulses, desires, ambitions and enthusiasm in the emotional, or what we shall in future call the psychic nature; and the intellect, ideality and perception, also the constructive and destructive element, in the mind, or mental nature.

II. *Taurus* (♉).—This is an earthy and fixed sign. Physically it governs the throat and neck. Psychically the secretive, lethargic and sensual feelings. Mentally, pride, endurance, stubbornness and the plodding tendencies.

III. *Gemini* (♊).—This is an airy and common or mutable sign. Physically it governs the lungs, arms and shoulders. Psychically, indecision, worry and anxiety. Mentally, nervousness, changeability, humour and versatility.

IV. *Cancer* (♋).—This is a watery and cardinal sign Physically it governs the breast and stomach. Psychicall,l the sensations, fancies, morbid tendencies and the materna sympathies. Mentally, economy, receptivity, memory and tenacity.

V. *Leo* (♌).—This is a fiery and fixed sign. Physically it governs the heart and back. Psychically the emotions, attractions, pride and generative passions. This is the centre of all the vital forces; as Aries governs the head and intellect, being the head of the fiery triplicity, so Leo governs the heart and the love nature, being the centre of the fiery signs. Mentally Leo expresses benevolence, liberality and kindness through thoughtfulness of heart.

VI. *Virgo* (♍).—This is an earthy and mutable sign. Physically it governs the bowels. Psychically the selfish, sensitive, bashful and adaptable feelings. Mentally, criticism analysis, logic and discrimination.

VII. *Libra* (♎).—This is an airy and cardinal sign. Physically it governs the groins and kidneys. Psychically the artistic and refined sympathies, approbativeness, and all social tendencies. Mentally, comparison, perception, judgment and equilibrium.

VIII. *Scorpio* (♏).—This is a watery and fixed sign. Physically it governs all the secret parts. Psychically the animal passions, secretiveness, jealousy and pride. Mentally, curiosity, mysticism, shrewdness, and power to judge accurately.

IX. *Sagittarius* (♐).—This is a fiery and mutable sign. Physically it governs the thighs. Psychically, restlessness, diffusiveness and the rebellious tendencies. Mentally, the prophetic, intuitive and philosophical.

X. *Capricorn* (♑).—This is an earthy and cardinal sign. Physically it governs the knees. Psychically, absorption, economy, perseverance and industry. Mentally, tact, diplomacy, ambition and practical thoroughness.

XI. *Aquarius* (♒).—This is an airy and fixed sign. Physically it governs the ankles. Psychically, the socialistic and convivial affections, faithfulness and sincerity. Mentally, the artistic, reasoning and contemplative tendencies.

XII. *Pisces* (♓).—This is a watery and mutable sign. Physically it governs the feet. Psychically the mediumistic, hospitable and romantic tendencies. Mentally it is impressionable, humane, methodical and indecisive.

It must be remembered that these descriptions are necessarily very brief and incomplete. Fuller descriptions of each sign will be found under their respective headings in *Everybody's Astrology*, and a still more extended explanation in *Astrology for All, Part I.*, where a detailed account is given of the "fate and fortune," in a general sense, of all persons born under each separate sign. But the above will be found sufficiently explicit for most purposes, and their conciseness renders them both easily available for reference and useful for comparison.

The twelve signs of the Zodiac are quite distinct from

the twelve houses. The Houses may be considered as the framework or skeleton, and literally represent all that is stationary and material, connected solely with the physical or concrete; the Signs may be thought of as the substance or covering of the twelve houses, the signs being the moving and active life of the houses and representing the psychic and plastic conditions governing the sensations, feelings and emotions; and as each sign of the zodiac has a lord or ruler in one of the planets, the Planets will therefore represent the mind or life of the whole. To emphasise this, these three factors may be thought of again as *cross*, *half-circle*, and *circle* respectively, the twelve Houses being formed on the *cross* of the cardinal points or the four 'angles' of the horoscope, the Signs of the zodiac in their two northern and southern halves being similar to the ever-changing *moon*, and the Planets wheeling round the zodiac as the *circle;* for it is practically true that in all astrological judgments the houses represent the body, the signs the animal soul, and the planets the mind or spirit.

The Houses of the Horoscope.—In reading a horoscope, then, we may for the purpose of judgment divide the map into *three* portions: (1) the twelve divisions called Houses representing the *body* or physical conditions (+); (2) the twelve Signs of the Zodiac the *soul*, or psychic and lower mental conditions (☽); and (3) the Planets, with the luminaries, the *spirit* or mind (○).

We may here make the distinction between *house* and *sign* which will apply to the various signs as we deal with them. The HOUSE shows fixed, radical or hereditary influences, while the SIGN indicates movable or personal influences; that which we inherit from our parents or environment will be shown by the twelve houses, but the inherent qualities which we possess or make for ourselves will be shown by the twelve signs of the zodiac. For instance, a malefic influence in the first house or ascendant will denote a severe early environment in which hardships will be endured over which the native has little or no control, while a benefic in Aries, the first sign of the zodiac, will show inherent capacity to affect surroundings and environment and so to change the fortunes as the opportunities offered are taken advantage of. This is only given as a general illustration.

The *houses* correspond to the *signs;* thus, the First House is in its nature similar to Aries, cardinal, aggressive, active, changeable, initiatory: and so on with the others, the Second House corresponding to Taurus, the Third to Gemini, etc.

The Signs and the Houses contrasted.—These may be distinguished in the mind in this way: Since the earth turns round on its axis once in twenty-four hours, it is clear that each house-cusp will pass through the whole circle of the zodiac once in a *day;* in the same way, the Sun passes through one sign a month, and so through the whole circle in a *year.* Hence we can have some idea of the ephemeral and comparatively trivial nature of the Houses, as compared with the Signs. While the former represent the limitations or opportunities appertaining to this life only, the latter relate to the sum-total of our previous experiences, powers which we have acquired by our own efforts in past lives. The planets, on the other hand, and their mutual relationships by aspect—benefic or malefic as the case may be—will represent the condition and evolutionary stage of the "Manas" or real part of ourselves that is at once the cause and the controller of our destiny. The periods of the planets are various, and therefore if, in order to fix our ideas, we compare the Houses and the Signs in their relation to the horoscope to the natural periods of the *day* and *year,* which recur in unvarying succession, we should have to regard the Planets as analogous to those cosmic periods of varying length and frequency which alternately remove or establish continents, which replace arid wastes by luxurious vegetation or *vice versâ*.

N.B.—The foregoing distinction is of the utmost importance and should never for a moment be lost sight of.

The Nature of the Twelve Houses.

I. The first house or Ascendant (*Eastern angle*) governs the head and personal qualities, such as environment, disposition and self-interest—in a word, *The Personality.*

II. The second house, financial affairs and monetary prospects, also the inspirational mind.

III. The third house, relatives, travel, and the general state of the *objective or lower* mind.

IV. The fourth house (*Northern angle*), residence, home life, parents, and the condition at the close of life.

V. The fifth house, pleasure, children, love affairs, and speculation.

VI. The sixth house, nature of sickness, servants, and psychic tendencies.

VII. The seventh house or Descendant (*Western angle*), marriage or business partner, and individual as distinguished from personal qualities—in a word, *The Individuality.*

VIII. The eighth house, wills, legacies, partner's financial conditions, *terminus vitæ;* or what is called death.

IX. The ninth house, philosophy, long journeys, foreign affairs and the general state of the *subjective or higher* mind.

X. The tenth house or Mid-heaven (*Southern angle*), profession, honours, ambitions and the general state of the moral conditions.

XI. The eleventh house, friends, acquaintances and hopes and wishes generally.

XII. The twelfth house, unseen troubles and misfortunes, emotional tendencies.

Notes and Comments.

(1) The terms "Personality" and "Individuality," as used above in connection with the first and seventh houses, require a word of explanation; for in Manual I. it was stated that these are represented respectively by the Moon and Sun. So they are, in a general way; but in any particular horoscope these two in a certain sense 'opposing' influences are severally focussed into the two houses in question. Viewed in this light, and bearing in mind what was said in the first manual as to the *meaning* of these two terms, as here used, a new and beautiful significance attaches to the common phrase so often applied to a husband or wife—"my better half." And just as the marriage partner supplies those physical, social, and spiritual qualities which the native externally lacks, embodying, as it were, in actuality those qualities he or she possesses only in latency, so the business partner will supply those mental and practical deficiencies for the want of which the native is unable to make the best use of his opportunities. The first and seventh houses may, in short, be looked upon as the two scale-pans of a balance, in which the objective and subjective elements in man are severally weighed. The thoughtful student of human nature will find much food for reflection in this suggestion.

(2) Following on this line of thought—and bearing in mind that we are here dealing with the houses alone, exclusive of the sign-positions of planets or the mutual aspects of the latter—the map may be divided into two portions, drawing a line from the first to the seventh (*horizon*). The part above the earth will represent the higher part of the nature, known as the individual or permanent self, representing the light or 'solar' half; and the part under the earth will symbolise the lower or

fleeting self, or that portion which is fettered by limitations, lacking opportunities and full expression, and thus called the unfortunate or dark and 'lunar' half.

(3) As has been said before, the houses 1, 4, 7, and 10, are known as the *cardinal* houses or 'angles'; they form a cross. The remaining houses form two other such crosses, known as *succedent* and *cadent*. They may be tabulated thus:—

Angular or cardinal	1	4	7	10
Succedent or fixed	2	5	8	11
Cadent or mutable	3	6	9	12

The "succedent" houses follow or succeed the angles, it will be seen, while the "cadent" fall away (Lat. *cado*) from the angles.

(4) The fact that there is a mutual *correspondence* between the Twelve Signs and the Twelve Houses, affords one a very useful clue when in doubt as to their meaning. For as the *signs* are to humanity at large, so are the *houses* to any particular individual: thus, Taurus, the second sign, represents the heritage of the human race, whether (*a*) physical, (*b*) intellectual, (*c*) social, or (*d*) moral; in precisely the same way the Second House indicates the heritage of the 'native,' his inherent good or bad fortune as expressed (*a*) in nutritiveness or alimentiveness, (*b*) essential mentality, as distinguished from intellectual ability, (*c*) social position at birth, (*d*) innate morality, *i.e.*, fixed tendencies or habits—in short, the *power of fixation*. This rule will be found of universal applicability, and will constantly prove of service in attempting to unravel the inner meaning of the horoscope.

We must now revert to the Signs of the Zodiac, of which it becomes necessary to make a detailed and analytical study.

TABLE OF SIGNS AND PLANETS.

	i	ii	iii	iv	v	vi	vii
	Sign	*Symbol*	*Ruling Planet*	*Sym. of Planet*	*Element*	*Quality**	*Exaltation*
Northern	1 ARIES	♈	Mars	♂	Fire	Cardinal *or* Movable	☉
	2 TAURUS	♉	Venus	♀	Earth	Fixed	☽
	3 GEMINI	♊	Mercury	☿	Air	Mutable *or* Common	
	4 CANCER	♋	Moon	☽	Water	Cardinal *or* Movable	♃
	5 LEO	♌	Sun	☉	Fire	Fixed	
	6 VIRGO	♍	Mercury	☿	Earth	Mutable *or* Common	
Southern	7 LIBRA	♎	Venus	♀	Air	Cardinal *or* Movable	♄
	8 SCORPIO	♏	Mars	♂	Water	Fixed	
	9 SAGITTARIUS	♐	Jupiter	♃	Fire	Mutable *or* Common	
	10 CAPRICORN	♑	Saturn	♄	Earth	Cardinal *or* Movable	♂
	11 AQUARIUS	♒	Saturn	♄	Air	Fixed	
	12 PISCES	♓	Jupiter	♃	Water	Mutable *or* Common	♀

* Where the letters C., F., M., are employed as abbreviations, as in Manual I., they imply the terms *cardinal, fixed* and *mutable*, respectively. The DETRIMENT of a planet is the opposite sign to its "house," and its FALL is the opposite to its "exaltation"; thus, ♈ is the detriment of ♀ and the fall of ♄.

Analysis of the Signs of the Zodiac.—On pp. 27 and 35 there are given two very useful tables of the twelve signs which the reader is recommended to study. It would require many volumes to explain the full nature of the signs of the Zodiac, but a very simple and easy method of understanding the Zodiac is to divide it into groups of signs, following our original plan of dividing the system into three portions. It will be noticed that there are three fiery, three earthy, three airy and three watery signs, and the whole twelve are again divided into three groups of cardinal, fixed and mutable, which we may tabulate as follows:—

Triplicities or Elements.

FIRE.	EARTH.	AIR.	WATER.
♈	♉	♊	♋
♌	♍	♎	♏
♐	♑	♒	♓

Quadruplicities or Qualities.

CARDINAL.	FIXED.	MUTABLE.
♈	♉	♊
♋	♌	♍
♎	♏	♐
♑	♒	♓

The Cardinal signs in the main govern the *head*, the Fixed signs the *trunk*, and the Mutable signs the *limbs* of the body. In a general sense the Cardinal signs govern the *mind or intellect*, the Fixed signs the *soul or will*, and the Mutable signs the *body or senses*. It is also important to remember that the signs are positive and negative (or male and female), in altenate order, thus:—

Positive	♈	♊	♌	♎	♐	♒
Negative	♉	♋	♍	♏	♑	♓

The following diagram indicates the location of the signs in the various parts of the body:—

THE TWELVE SIGNS OF THE ZODIAC

And their relation to the Human Anatomy according to Ancient Astrology.

Head and Face ♈

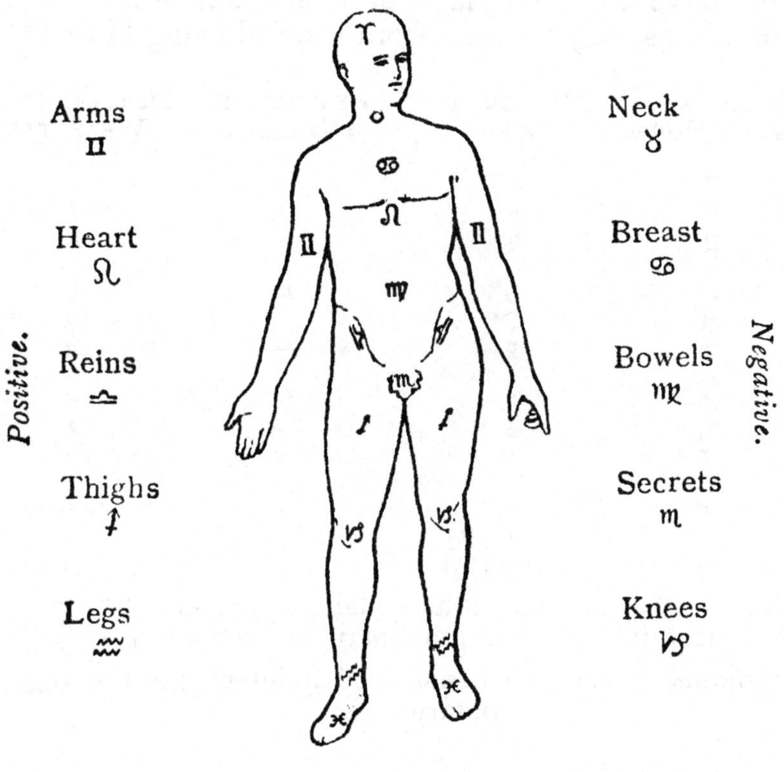

Feet ♓

"Every physical organisation in the elemental world—be it atom, man or universe—comprehends a polar zodiac, the twelve divisions of which are but different powers or functions of the One Law. On every plane of manifestation—be it mineral, vegetable, or animal—these divisions correspond respectively in vibration, and are therefore analogous in principle and attunement. 'As is the Macrocosm so is the Microcosm'—as is the higher, so is the lower."

Planets as Rulers of the Twelve Signs.—Each sign has a lord or ruler, the sign being a vehicle or form for the planet's expression. It is therefore necessary to know the ruler of each sign, also the signs in which certain planets have their strength or exaltation, weakness or detriment, as may be seen from the following table:

SIGN *or* PLANET'S HOUSE	RULER *or* LORD	EXALTATION *or* STRENGTH	DETRIMENT *or* WEAKNESS
♈	♂	☉	♀
♉	♀	☽	♂
♊	☿	—	♃
♋	☽	♃	♄
♌	☉	—	♄
♍	☿	—	♃
♎	♀	♄	♂
♏	♂	—	♀
♐	♃	—	☿
♑	♄	♂	☽
♒	♄ (♅)	(☿)	☉
♓	♃ (♆)	♀	☿

The positive or 'masculine' planets are:—☉ ♂ ♃ ♅.
The negative or 'feminine' planets are:—☽ ♀ ♄ ♆.
The planet ☿ may be considered indeterminate as regards polarity of sex.

The Influence of the Planets.—If for the purpose of understanding the nature of the planets, without going into the region of metaphysics, we consider the terms Good and Evil as relative only, we shall quickly understand how their influences will operate fortunately or unfortunately as rulers over our fate and destiny.

THE SUN is the positive life-giving centre ever giving forth the vital principle, and from a physical standpoint governing the constitution and organic portion of the human system, having thus a dual influence in what may be termed life and spirit.

THE MOON is the negative receiver and collector of all the influences or vibrations of the Sun and Planets, physically governing all the functional arrangements in the human system, and the formative and plastic side of existence.

MERCURY, being neither positive nor negative, but convertible, and acting as the Messenger of the Gods, will as it were contain in itself both the solar and lunar expressions, manifesting one or the other or both in the specifically human attributes, and physically governing the nervous system.

In this division we see again the three manifested as Father, Mother, Child ; or positive, negative, and neutral or dual principle ; and now we may by a study of these three obtain a clearer understanding as to the nature of the planets.

The Circle Explained.—The ○ is the main central principle of ♂ and ♀, the circle being under the cross in the case of Mars, and over the cross in the symbol of Venus. In one case, life or spirit is dominated by matter, and expresses the passional and forceful side of life, the + over ○ denoting that the objective side of life will be manifested wherever Mars is prominent in a nativity—the good being expressed by Mars on the side of energy and activity, and the evil by force and passion, or the abuse of the desire-nature, according to the aspects and sign- or house-position of Mars. The circle over the cross in the case of Venus symbolises the conquest of spirit over matter, or life over form, and the turning of the passions and external senses inward to feeling and sympathy, beauty and appreciation. The circle, as the symbol of love and perfection, shows the three modes of expression according to the symbol. The Sun (☉) as universal love, Venus (♀) as human love, and Mars (♂) as animal passion. In reading the horoscope these three factors must be taken into consideration when dealing with love and marriage or life and general success, as expressing the destiny side of the nativity.

The Half-Circle Explained.—We shall now consider the three symbols connected with the half-circle. The Moon is the central agent in all matters connected with the psychic and negative side of the nature; it represents the intermediate stage between the purely objective and subjective states; it governs the personal or more limited side of manifestation; and it is the principal ruler over fate, when considered in connection with Saturn and Jupiter, the former having the half-circle under the cross, and the latter the half-circle over the cross. Saturn denotes limitation and labour, hardships and privation, sorrow and obstruction, and is thus called the Greater Misfortune. Jupiter denotes the reverse of Saturn, the psychic nature having risen above the cross of matter, thus indicating expansion and freedom, ease and comfort, joy and liberation.

The Combined Influence.—The next influence toconsider is that of Mercury, whose symbol contains the three, cross, half-circle and circle combined. This is the lord of the body and the ruler of the mind. All complete forms are under the influence of Mercury, and all bodies on all planes are moulded by his influence, therefore this planet is in itself only the vehicle or expression of the life manifesting according to the horoscope. On either side of Mercury we have Uranus and Neptune as positive and negative representatives of Mercury. The vibrations of these planets are only just beginning to be felt by the present race, but the coming sixth race will be more fitted to express the influence of Uranus and Neptune than the great majority of to-day.

It will now be seen that the ☉, the ☽ and ☿ form the central three, representing the Spirit, Soul, and Body. By setting these out in tabular form a more clear understanding may be obtained as to their value when reading the horoscope.

Subjective.	*Neutral.*	*Objective.*
♀ Love	☉ Spirit or Life Principle	♂ Energy and Passion
♃ Expansion	☽ Reception and Collection	♄ Limitation and Contraction
♅ Regeneration	☿ Memory and Reflection	♆ Fancy and Impression

Nature of the Aspects.—On p. 21 it was shown how the aspects were calculated, and it is now time to describe their nature; for before the horoscope can be read the aspects of the planets to one another, and the position of the latter, both by *house* and by *sign*, their strength also and their weakness, must all be known.

When the aspects are formed from the same triplicity they are harmonious; but when formed out of the triplicities and from uncongenial signs they are inharmonious. Two planets in different *fiery* signs, such as ♈ and ♌ or ♌ and ♐, for instance, will be in trine aspect, which is favourable; the same when both planets are in signs of the *earthy* triplicity, and similarly with the *watery* and *airy* triplicities.

But when aspects are formed from signs of the same Cardinal, Fixed or Mutable group they are unfavourable. The Cardinal group is made up of the four elements, so that a planet in ♈ and another in ♋ will be in a more or less close square aspect: and it will be seen that fire and water do not agree. This is the rule when judging the nature of all the aspects. Earthy and watery signs are in sextile, and as earth and water will blend the aspect is favourable; but fire and earth have no sympathy, although fire and air have; and so on. A little practice is necessary to know the aspects at a glance, but their general nature may be seen from this table:—

SYMBOL.	NAME.	NATURE.	FORMED IN.
△	Trine	Benefic	Signs of same *triplicity*
□	Square	Malefic	,, ,, *quality*
✱	Sextile	Good	Fire *and* air, or earth *and* water
∠	Semi-quadrate	Evil	45° distant
⚼	Sesqui-quadrate	,,	135° distant
⚺	Semi-sextile	Doubtful	One sign distant
⚻	Quincunx	,,	Five signs distant
☌	Conjunction	(*See note*)	In same sign
☍	Opposition	Unfavourable	In opposite signs

In regard to the exact nature of the aspects, only experience can really teach. But the most helpful suggestion that can be given the student is to work out in his mind the analogy of the aspects with the houses: thus, the △ is a "fifth house" or a "ninth house" aspect, according as the quicker planet is separating from, or approaching towards, the slower; and so on with the others. It is for this reason that the ∠ and ⚼ are so anomalous in their nature, since they correspond to *half-way through a house:* hence they are of a generally worrying nature but bring little to pass, good or evil.

Note.—The conjunction will be good or evil, according to the nature of the planets forming the conjunction.

CPSIA information can be obtained
at www.ICGtesting.com
Printed in the USA
LVOW03s2123180716
496836LV00001B/7/P